Winter Survival Guide:
20 Proven Lessons To Survive A Winter Storm

Table of content

Introduction

The winter storm has always been a part of winter. To be classed as a genuine winter storm there must be extreme weather which causes risk to human live and of damage to property. Although it has always happened there are many who believe there are an increasing number of them in recent years. In fact, the last few winters have barely seen one week go by without a storm somewhere in the world. The effects of these storms can be devastating; houses can be destroyed, whole communities can even suffer.

Of course, storms do happen in the spring and the fall; with even the odd summer storm. But, the major difference between these storms and the winter ones is the danger to your life after the storm has passed. Winter is traditionally a time of freezing conditions; this can cause serious issues after the storm has passed. Cold is one of the biggest killers and if you are not properly prepared it could be you which suffers.

There are a variety of different types of storm which can arrive at this time of year and whilst the preparations are generally the same it is useful to know what kind of storm may be about to hit you. You should receive adequate warning via the weather forecast and the local news channel, but it is always worth keeping an eye on the internet and activities in other parts of the world. A storm usually starts somewhere and works its way across the country; if you are not at the starting point you may be able to track it and have more time to prepare.

Snow storms can cause huge amounts of disruption as they will blind and disorientate you. However the biggest risk in these is the weight of huge amounts of snow falling; this can damage the roofs of buildings and threaten lives. On top of this is the temperature stays low the snow will not melt and there will be snow drifts and ice issues. An additional issue if you are in the mountains is the risk of an avalanche. Once the snowstorm has passed you may experience flooding; if the level of snow is high this can cause serious issues of its own.

If conditions are cold enough you can also experience an ice storm; this is when it rains ice or hail stones and you are left dealing with damage from freezing power lines, icy roads and multiple accidents. An ice storm can cause far more damage than a snow storm.

Of course the worst storms are those that include high winds. These can take the roof of a building off, bring trees down and lift vehicles into the air. When you combine strong winds with a winter storm you can experience wide spread devastation. The issue is not always about surviving the actual storm; this can often be the easier part.   When widespread damage happens to property and infrastructure it can takes weeks, months or even years to return everything to normal. This period of time can be extremely difficult to survive as there will be poor sanitation and a potential lack of electricity, food and even water. Being prepared for this will ensure you survive and even flourish during this period!

Chapter 1 – 5 Strategies to prepare for a Winter Storm

Even if you live in an area which does not often experience winter storms it is important to consider how a serious storm could affect you if it were to happen. This must be the first step in realizing the importance of preparing yourself for a storm. The following five strategies should all be adopted to ensure you are fully prepared for any kind of winter storm.

These strategies assume you are expecting to be stuck at home or are in your vehicle.

1. The Emergency Kit

The first strategy is to create an emergency sack. The following items should be stored somewhere safe at home and easy to access. You can also keep a smaller version of this kit in your vehicle in case you are stuck in a snow storm and unable to get to your house or another place of safety. Of course, if you are aware the storm is coming you are better not traveling unless essential.

- Water – The recommended amount is one gallon of water per person who will be sheltering with you. You should have at least three day's supply; this means if there are four of you then you will need twelve gallons of water.

- You should be able to estimate how much food you and your family generally consume. You can then store enough for your family to survive at least three days. It is important that this food does not perish; you will need canned food or dried products and possibly a means to cook the items; such as a gas camping stove. It is essential to put at least one can opener with your tins!

- Battery operated radio and spare batteries.

- Torch and more spare batteries.

- A comprehensive first aid kit; bandages, plasters, dressings and antiseptic cream at the very least.

- A whistle and possibly some flares to notify any search parties.

- Garbage bags; these can be used for a variety of purposes.

- Basic tools such as a wrench to stop water leaks.

- Blankets to help keep everyone warm. You can even have spare clothes available.

- A cell phone charger and possibly even a spare cell phone. IT is worth considering having a solar operated cell phone charger.

- Maps of the local area to assist in locating streams and other natural resources.

2. Shelter

http://ichef.bbci.co.uk/news/624/media/images/80112000/jpg/_80112625_5a704472-5092-4803-aa34-f299b650f53c.jpg

The most important part of immediate survival is having somewhere safe to go. If you are in your home you will probably be inclined to stay there. However, there are a few points which should be considered:

- Safety – which part of your home is most likely to survive high winds? A basement is usually a safe bet although you will also need to assess the risk of flooding during or after the storm. As well as creating your emergency store in the safest part of the house you will need to consider the possible exits in case one is blocked.

- A winter storm may result in a loss of electricity and gas. You should choose an alternative heat source and keep it with your emergency supplies; checking it regularly to ensure it works. Of course, a kerosene heater can be dangerous if there is not sufficient ventilation; you must ensure there is airflow in your shelter.

- Your safety shelter should be limited in size; just one room of your house is adequate. This is to make it easier to heat. You should also be aware of how many windows are in the room and have wood prepared to block them at night to keep the heat in. This can also be used if your windows are broken.

- You will need to consider sleeping arrangements and a toilet area; if you are unable to access the rest of your home. These do not have to be spectacular but you will need something. Remember it is unlikely you will have running water so a composting toilet or simple garbage bags may be the only method available.

3. Watching

The next important strategy is to be aware. This means watching the news, weather reports and any other relevant information you can find on the internet. This should not become obsessive! You should locate a trustworthy internet source and check it regularly. Watching the news and the weather daily will help you to stay up to date with any potential storms arriving.

Combining the three different approaches and learning to read between the lines should ensure you are ready before a storm arrives; even if a public announcement has not been made by the government.

There are other signs which are important to watch during the winter. Your forecast should indicate the wind chill; it is usually labeled advisory, watch or warning. When there is a wind chill warning you can accept very cold strong winds. These will combine with the cold weather to create extreme cold where it is easily possible to hypothermia, frostbite or even die from cold exposure.

There will also be a freeze warning which tells you that the surface temperature will be at or very close to freezing. This can be lethal to young children, the elderly, pets and crops. Combined with a wind chill warning it can be lethal.

4. *Prepare your Home*

http://www.quickanddirtytips.com/sites/default/files/styles/insert_medium/public/images/7656/winterstorm.jpg?itok=jYQoqi9N

Super strong winds which can rip your roof off are extremely difficult to protect against. All you can really do is ensure your property is maintained regularly and all repairs are done as quickly as possible.

However, the extreme cold that usually accompanies a winter storm can be a range of other issues. These can be protected against.

The first thing to consider is protecting your pipes. Although it is likely that the water supply will be cut off, you will not want the water which is in the pipes freezing and damaging your pipes. If your house survives the storm then you will be upset to find it flooded once the water supply returns! As well as insulating the pipes you should keep the thermostat in your home set at 60 Fahrenheit. This will help to prevent the pipes from freezing, as will allowing your faucets to drip slowly; moving water is harder to freeze!

As well as having a heating source in your emergency kit you should consider having a generator and some candles; this can make a difference to your comfort when waiting out a storm or surviving after one.

It is also essential to secure all windows and doors, draughts will be magnified in a winter storm making it more difficult to heat your house and glass can easily break. Shutters fitted securely to the outside of your home can make a huge difference to your warmth and security during a storm.

5. Communication System

The final step to being prepared for any winter storm is ensuring you have a communication system and a plan established. It is highly likely that the telephone lines will be affected in a winter storm; even the cell towers can be damaged. You may be able to use a satellite phone; however this is an expensive option to keep in an emergency kit and probably not something you would wish to use as your everyday phone!

The alternative is either short range radios; enabling you to communicate with loved ones in the close vicinity. Or, you can purchase a ham radio. This will need an antenna to help broadcast far enough and your loved ones will need similar equipment. Fortunately this is not expensive although it does require you to have a license before you are legally allowed to operate one.

Alongside proper communication equipment it is essential to devise your plan before you need it. The key element of any plan is knowing who will be at your house and how they will get there in the event of a storm. Ideally you will have enough warning for everyone to get to your house; if not then it is important to have considered a contingency plan.

Chapter 2 – 5 Essential Strategies When You Are Trapped Outside

The ability to survive a storm is much easier when you are in your own home and have your pre-prepared supplies with you. However, despite the best of intentions it is possible that you will find yourself stuck outside when a winter storm hits. This may be because the storm is unexpected, you are on a road trip, or even camping and have not received a warning. Whatever the reason, an important part of surviving is developing a strategy to handle being stuck outside in a winter storm.

1. Shelter

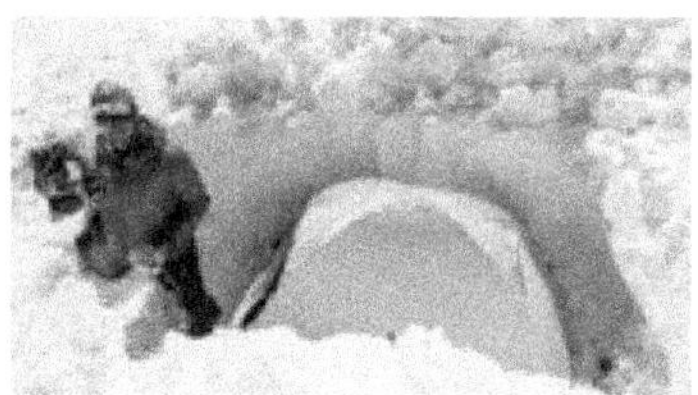

https://i.kinja-img.com/gawker-media/image/upload/s--Wzn8NpDH--/c_scale,f_auto,fl_progressive,q_80,w_800/vlmxso1t1uwvtfssp1za.jpg

It is unlikely that you will be immediately hungry or thirsty as you will have been eating and drinking normally prior to the storm arriving. This means that you do not have a desperate need for food or water. What you do need is a shelter. The extreme cold of a storm and the aftermath can quickly lower your core temperature to dangerous levels; resulting in hypothermia or even death. In this sort of situation minutes can literally make the difference between life and death.

There are a variety of possibilities regarding the shelter; it is unlikely you will have much time if you are caught in a storm. A cave is one of the best options, however an alternative is simple to burrow into the ground and cover yourself over; with leaves if possible but if not you can use snow. Despite the fact that this will make you wet and cold it will not reduce your body temperature as drastically or as quickly as if you stay in the wind.

It is also possible to build a snow cave if you have time. This involves making a huge pile of snow and then burying into the middle of it. The entrance should be as small as possible and there should be an air hole in the roof. It is also best to set the entrance at an angle so you are going uphill into the cave.

2. Clothing

If you are prepared for a storm then you will have multiple thin layers of clothing on; this is one of the best ways of staying warm in any type of colder weather. If you do get wet and are unable to change your clothes you need to create a fire if possible. Whilst this is easy in a home situation you will need to find something to burn and a means of lighting it in the wild. A lighter would be idea but if not then you will need to practice rubbing sticks together. It would be best to practice this before you find yourself in a survival situation.

If you have created a snow cave or found a shelter which you can use before planning your next move you will be able to dry your clothes simply by hanging them in the cold air. Providing the storm has passed, the cold can dry your clothes surprisingly quickly and help you to stay warm!

3. Water

You cannot survive more than a few days without water. It is essential to find some as soon as the storm allows you to exit your temporary shelter. This is also the opportunity to assess the situation around you and decide what your next move is. This will depend upon whether you know where you are and how far civilization is; it will also depend on whether the storm has passed or is likely to return.

Although in a winter storm you may be surrounded by snow or ice, you cannot drink this even thought it should be fairly pure. The main reason for this is that ice cold water will need to be heated by your body; this will need to be done by your body. The effort of doing this will actually cause you to lose heat; although you will stay hydrated! The better solution is to place the snow in a container and heat it by placing it next to a fire or near your body without being in direct contact. Once it has warmed it will be okay to drink without affecting your body temperature.

4. Cover Up

Whether you are in a cave, snow cave or even trying to stay warm in your car it is essential to keep yourself wrapped up. You will lose as much as sixty percent of your heat through your head and neck. If you do not have a hat you should wrap another item of clothing around your head and neck to protect them. You should also keep your hands and feet covered. The colder your body gets the more it will focus on keeping your vital organs warm. This means that blood flow to the extremities will be reduced. Keeping them covered will help them and you to stay warm. It is much easier to stay warm than it is to try and get warm after having become cold. It is also advisable to do light exercise such as stomping your feet; opening and closing your hands or even clapping. However, you should avoid doing strenuous exercise unless it is essential. Heavy exercise will make you sweat and in extreme conditions this can turn to frost against your skin; which can decrease your core temperature and even result in frost bite.

5. Entertainment

http://bloximages.newyork1.vip.townnews.com/richmond.com/content/tncms/assets/v3/editorial/b/3f/b3f826bc-6049-11e3-8b6a-0019bb30f31a/52a4da75eabdf.image.jpg?resize=760%2C501

Being trapped outside in a temporary shelter with little or no food and water waiting for a storm to pass is demoralizing. It is very easy to become negative about the situation. It will usually start by dwelling on the items which you should have had prepared and carried with you and can lead to a doom and gloom outlook. However, this is the worst thing you can do! Instead focus on positive images and the things you intend to do next in your life. Not only will these lift your spirits and help you to find a solution it will also help the storm appear to pass quicker. Once it has passed you will be able to assess the situation and decide on the best course of action depending on where you are and what damage the storm has caused.

Keeping yourself entertained can be as simple as singing to yourself or playing puzzles in your head; really anything that takes your mind off your current situation will help. If you have found shelter and wrapped up as warm as possible there is little else you can do until the storm has passed.

Chapter 3 – 5 Strategies for Staying Alive After the Storm

There is generally little you can do once the storm has arrived; other than baton down the hatches and wait it out. Providing you have managed to prepare the basics you should be able to focus on passing the time instead of waiting for the storm to finish. However, the biggest part of surviving a severe winter storm is actually after the storm has passed. You must be sure that it has passed before you venture out; storms generally have an eye when it goes extremely calm before it starts again!

Merging from your shelter you may found there is extensive damage to property, power lines and other utilities. The first thing you will need to do is check your own shelter; if it is damaged you will need to assess whether you can or should fix it at this stage. If it is not detrimental to your survival efforts you may be better to leave it. The following strategies should help you to survive the aftermath and await the utilities being repaired.

1. *Your Roof*

http://www.brimg.net/images/man-shoveling-snow-off-of-house-roof_573x300.jpg

You may be surprised at just how heavy snow and ice can be. After a winter storm it is important to clear your roof as soon as possible to prevent any undue stress being placed on the roof of your structure. If you do not, further snowfall can cause your roof to collapse.

You must take care when clearing the roof; ladders and brushes are essential and the assistance of another family member will help to ensure your safety.

It is advisable to keep a variety of tools which will help with this sort of task in a secure spot ready for when you may need them. This will ensure this task can be completed quickly.

2. *The Local Area*

You will think that you already know your local area but, it may look different after a storm and your current attention is probably not on the things which will matter in the aftermath of a storm.

You should work out where the local water sources are as this may be an important means of staying alive. Alongside this it is important to consider what routes may become snow bounded, flooded or destroyed and how else you may be able to get around. You will need to assume that the car will no longer be an option; if it is then it will be a bonus!

3. Food

http://files.harrispublications.com/wp-content/uploads/sites/5/2015/12/winter-storm-food-supply-661x441.jpg

The aim before the storm was to have enough food stockpiled to last you for three days. This will certainly see you through most storms; however, it will not be enough to help you if the utilities and infrastructure are damaged. You may also find that it is not as simple as popping to the local shop; even if you still have money to pay for items.

You should, therefore, decide the best place to source food locally. This may be through hunting in the local forest or in the streams and sea near your home. You may even grow food for your own consumption and be able to use some of this. There will also be an abundance of berries and nuts in the vicinity; providing you know what and where to look. Familiarize yourself with these things now to help if a storm hits.

4. Safety

Unfortunately when the infrastructure breaks down it is likely that you will find people taking the law into their own hands; the principle of survival of the fittest is often quoted. In truth it is survival of those who are most prepared. You may need to keep your house or shelter looking like it is not being used to avoid attracting attention. It is also advisable to keep a knife or even a firearm in reserve for occasions like this. Whilst you will hopefully not need to use these items if it is ever necessary to protect your family you should not hesitate.

5. Alternate Location

If your house or shelter is damaged or if the area has simply become too dangerous then you should consider what other location may be better for you. It is best to work this out before you are faced with a storm. You may have or know of a small piece of land on which you can create a den and equip it with the basic survival materials. This should not be too far from your own home to ensure you can keep an eye on it before it is needed. It will also need to be accessible in the aftermath of the storm. There is, of course, no way of guaranteeing that you will be able to get to your alternate location but the more you consider storm forces before you build it the more likely it is to still be standing!

Chapter 4 – Alternate Survival Strategies

If a severe winter storm does affect the area you live in then hopefully you will have followed the advice in this book and be safely in a shelter, waiting for the storm to pass and ready for whatever happens after this. Of course, it is rare for everything to go as you plan; no matter how good your planning is. It is during these occasions that a range of alternate survival strategies can be brought into play. The following simple measures can literally help to save your life if you are caught out in a winter storm:

1. Cardboard

https://dsx.weather.com//util/image/v/snow__172517.jpg?v=at&w=485&h=273&api=7db9fe61-7414-47b5-9871-e17d87b8b6a0

You may have heard of homeless people who line their clothes with newspaper to help retain their body heat on cold winter nights. This is actually a proven fact; paper is an excellent form of insulation. If you are stuck outside trying to get to a shelter or in a shelter then you can wrap yourself with card board; or even line your body with paper. The additional layer of 'clothing' will insulate your body; allowing you to retain your body heat.

This can also be effective if you are at home and the power has gone. Without power you may not have a heat source; the temperature will drop surprisingly quickly. When inside your house you can resort to building a cardboard fort in one room and moving you and your family inside it; it will act as excellent insulation and help to keep you all warm. You may be surprised at just how effective it is!

2. Elevate Yourself

The ground is cold at the best of times and even more so when you have a winter storm billowing around you. The combination of snow, ice and freezing winds will chill the ground beneath you instantly. Unfortunately if you are in contact with the ground it will literally suck the heat from your body; leaving you at risk of hypothermia and death. One of the most important ways to stay warm in the outdoors is to elevate yourself from the ground. Standing on logs can help or building yourself a mossy surface will lift your feet from the cold ground.

This is even more important if you need to sleep; lying down on the ground will rapidly reduce your core body temperature. Anything which elevates you and preferably creates an air pocket between you and the ground will ensure you stay much warmer. Even inside a building you should adhere to this principle. If there is no bed available then use any other furniture or items that you can find; it will make a difference.

3. *Be Together*

One thing which is almost guaranteed to ensure you take unnecessary and life threatening risks is when your group becomes separated and you are trying to locate one of them. It is essential that everyone knows how the plan works during and after a winter storm. This will ensure you know where everyone should be and you can keep everyone together. Staying in one place also means that you will find it easy to keep everyone hydrated and warm whilst you wait for the storm to pass.

This is even more important if you are stranded outside. During a winter storm being outside can easily cause you to become disorientated. If you are in a group you should find or make a temporary shelter and huddle together until the storm has finished. Even after it has passed it is best to stay together whilst you evaluate your next step.

4. *Hot Drinks*

http://i.dailymail.co.uk/i/pix/2014/12/21/242AFFA800000578-2883005-image-m-33_1419204985820.jpg

Many people believe that one way of staying warm is to drink plenty of hot drinks. However, a hot drink will warm you mentally but have very little effect physically; although it will help you to stay hydrated. However, a hot liquid is a very good way to dissolve sugar and get it into your body. Sugar can be burnt by your muscles to create energy and heat; both processes will help you to stay warm. Sugar is also very easy to keep in your emergency kit. It is better to consume it in a liquid form to allow it to rapidly be absorbed by your body although simply eating sugar will help if you have no other option.

The energy boost can also be useful to help you stay awake and focused through a storm. Although it can be worth considering sleeping through a storm it is generally agreed to be safer to stay awake and be ready to react to any issue.

5. Transport

Just prior to a storm hitting you will usually hear a warning issued by the government. This can be the trigger to jump in your car and head for somewhere else. However, unless you have somewhere specific to go and it is unlikely to be in the path of the storm, you may be better off staying where you are. A car will give limited protection from the cold and, if there are many people trying to flee you could simply end up trying to wait out a storm in your vehicle; which is not a desirable option.

Instead, you should consider keeping your vehicle inside if possible; this will reduce the chances of it becoming damaged during the storm and you may be able to use it after the storm has passed.

Conclusion

A winter storm can be deadly. There are many people killed every year who are simply not prepared for the storm and the aftermath. Whilst the elderly and young children are at most risk, this type of extreme weather can affect anyone.

Being prepared will increase your chances of surviving. In particular it will help you to sort your resources and make a plan after the storm has passed. When the infrastructure is damaged and will take weeks or longer to repair many people will die from sanitation issues or simply lack of food. Thinking about the options and the best method of survival now is essential. You can develop a plan, but, more importantly you will be aware of the options and the important facts which can make a huge difference to your chance of survival.

The difficulty faced by anyone trying to survive is that you do not know what will be damaged and what will not. Equally it is impossible to accurately predict how much damage a storm will do; you may find yourself preparing for something which does not happen. However, this is preferably to not preparing yourself and finding yourself without any resources in the middle of an extreme winter storm.

The frequency of these types of events is on the increase; there are many theories regarding why this is the case but the most important fact is that storms are a real threat and something you should plan for them now. There are many possible options depending upon where you are when a storm hits but the strategies presented in this book are true for any storm or even for other types of disasters such as nuclear warfare. Surviving the actual storm or incident is often much easier than surviving the aftermath. This can be a much more dangerous time as the normal structure of society is surprisingly fragile and can collapse when the normal parameters are rapidly altered.

Even after the storm has passed it is important to exercise extreme caution, a hint of sunshine does not mean the temperature has warmed up and there is likely to be icy surfaces which can cause serious injury. This is part of the reason why it is so important to have several days' worth of water and food; even if the infrastructure has not been seriously damaged you may find that you are unable to travel. Providing your home has escaped unscathed and you have followed the preparations in this book you will be comfortable waiting for the utilities to b restored and for you to be able to get out and about again.

FREE Bonus Reminder

If you have not grabbed it yet, please go ahead and download your special bonus E book *"Chakras for Beginners. 7 Steps To Understand And Balance Chakras, Radiate Energy, And Strengthen Aura"*.

Simply Click the Button Below

OR Go to This Page

http://lifehacksworld.com/free

BONUS #2: More Free & Discounted Books & Products

Do you want to receive more Free/Discounted Books or Products?

We have a mailing list where we send out our new Books or Products when they go free or with a discount on Amazon. Click on the link below to sign up for Free & Discount Book & Product Promotions.

=> Sign Up for Free & Discount Book & Product Promotions <=

OR Go to this URL

http://zbit.ly/1WBb1Ek